The Olden Days of Long Ago

memory poems

by Rick Lanoue

Copyright © 2023 David G. Lanoue

ISBN 978-1-7333016-5-7
New Orleans, Louisiana
HaikuGuy.com

Edited by David G. Lanoue, Rick's brother
Source material: Debbie Boyle, Rick's sister
Back cover photography: Tim Boyle, Rick's brother-in-law

The Olden Days of Long Ago

memory poems

INTRODUCTION

My older brother Richard Joseph Lanoue, born on October 6, 1947, had a phenomenal memory. Tell him your birthday and he would remember it always. Once, in sixth or maybe seventh grade (my memory isn't as sharp as Rick's), I brought three pals from school home to meet him—just once. Over forty years later, I asked him if he remembered Jim Chess, Mike Gaffney, and John Ward. He not only remembered them; he remembered and recited their birthdays.

Confined to a wheelchair his whole life due to cerebral palsy, Rick had the use of one hand with one typewriter-pecking index finger, which he put to good use, recording hundreds of pages of memories. In later years, he lost the use of that hand and finger, sadly ending both his writing career and his ability to play Christmas songs on his electric chord organ.

Not long after his 76th birthday, he fell sick. His doctor at first thought it was pneumonia, but a body scan abruptly changed the diagnosis to stage four colon cancer. I rushed to Omaha to spend three days with him—the first at his hospital room in Intensive Care, the next two at his hospital-adjacent nursing home. Big brother was in bad shape; he couldn't talk couldn't even will his facial muscles to smile. This was really sad, because Rick usually had an earnest, generous smile that could light up any room.

I told him how years ago I had taken four of the memories that he had typed long ago and laid them out on the page as short little poems. I had initially thought to put together a book but later (I can't remember why) abandoned this project. I had recently come across these four "found poems" while clearing out my office at my university.

I read these four snippets from his *History of the Family* to Rick. Would he like to publish a book of memories in poetic form to give to friends and family? (He blinked for "Yes.") Would he like his name to appear in the book as Richard Joseph Lanoue? (He closed his eyes for "No.") Rick Lanoue, then? (He blinked).

Rick loved Christmas. Every year since 1967 he hosted a family Christmas show—for most years in the basement rec room of our home in Omaha but during and since the Covid pandemic, via Zoom. I suggested to him that he might give this book to relatives and friends as a Christmas present. Would he like that? (Firm blink.)

Rick didn't live to see this collection of his memories. A few days after our conversation, he passed away—on November 4, 2023.

So here they are: words he wanted to share about his olden days, age ten to thirty-five. Rick Lanoue's Christmas present for the world.

THE YEAR of 1957

I WENT TO CAMP

Mom took Debbie
to the hospital
on the 21st of February
in 1957

and it was on Thursday
night when Grandma Knight
was here

then she had
a bloody throat too

I went to camp with the kids
that used to go to school
at Dr. Lord's
when they were young

but the last day of camp
was so windy
and it was Mom's birthday

then she got
a radio

MY TOOTH

I fell out of the wheelchair
and I bumped my tooth
by fiddling around
with the handle
of the big gray safe
in the Physical Therapy room

on Tuesday afternoon
in 1957
but it was on the 15th
of October

then it was on a clear day
right after
the rest period
of the old Dr. J. P. Lord School
building

I was ten years old
and I cried
because it was hurting

so Dad took me
to the dentist
to put a silver cap
on that night
before suppertime
when Grandma Knight
was here

THE YEAR of 1959

I HELD JANELLE

I held Janelle when she
was a little baby
on Easter Day
in 1959

then it was on Sunday
morning

but the date
for that day was on
the 29th of March
so Debbie held my left arm

and I wore braces
on that day too

MY LEFT KNEE CAP

I hurt my left knee cap
by walking to my wheelchair

on the 28th of April
in 1959

and it was on Tuesday morning
but it was so clear

on that day
too

I SQUIRTED DAVID

I squirted David
with a backyard
garden hose

when he was
in the swimming pool

on the 27th of June
in 1959

then he started
to cry

after two Debbies
splashed some water
at him

but he came out
of the swimming pool

on Saturday afternoon
so it was so cloudy

on that day too

THE 4th OF JULY

Mom took a picture of Dad
sleeping on the couch

and Debbie woke him up
in the livingroom

then she said
come on in
lip reading in the kitchen

on the 4th of July
in 1959

Dad and I went
on the rolling coaster
then we went
on the helicopters

but we rode in the cars
so we rode on the train
at Peony Park

we went over to the Hines's
for homemade ice cream too

and it was so good
then we went home

we went to Iowa City
in Iowa
and Grandma Knight
went with us

but my parents took me
to the hospital
for a clinic

then the doctor came in
so we went on a picnic

Dad fastened Janelle
with a belt of his
to the seat of the swing
at the park

so she stayed on
when she was a little girl
in Iowa City

then he pushed me
on the bridge
when I was a little boy too

we started heading back
and we saw
a rainbow

Debbie and Leslie
were dressed alike
by wearing the same clothes

when we got home
from the trip
to Iowa City in Iowa

so Mom took a picture
of Loretta
when she went home

then she borrowed a cup
of sugar

I STARTED SCHOOL

I started school
on the 9th of September
in 1959

at Dr. J. P. Lord School
and I was in
third grade then

I had Mrs. Radenbaugh
for a third grade teacher

but it was so clear
on that day

David started school
at Benson West
and it was on Wednesday

then Janelle
got the plastic car
with a mouse
that goes squeak
when she squeezed it

but Dad brought it home
for her
so they took a picture
of her toy
too

FIRST COMMUNION

Debbie and I
made the first communion

on the 24th of October
in 1959

but she kissed me first
then I kissed her

on the 25th of October
in 1959

on Sunday so Mom
gave us our prayer book

even the rosary
too

David was sick
on that day too

and we went
to Leslie Badura's
birthday party

even me too

ROOM SIXTEEN

I was in room sixteen
at Dr. J. P. Lord School

on the 17th of December
in 1959

and I came on the stage
in Civic Auditorium too

then it was our turn
to be on the stage

as wisemen

BOB LICKERT

Bob Lickert dressed
like a Santa Claus
and he came
on Christmas Eve

but the date for that day
was on the 24th
of December in 1959

and it was on Thursday
night too

so David said
that it was Bob Lickert

then I
agreed with him
too

THE YEAR of 1960

MOM WAS SLIDING

Mom was sliding

and one of her shoes
fell off

on the 2nd of January
in 1960

but it was on Saturday
afternoon

then it was so cloudy
on that day too

PORKY PIG

I watched the cartoon
about Porky Pig
when he refused to learn
I pledge allegiance

on the 22nd of February
in 1960
lots of times
on the TV set

and it
was on Monday
afternoon

FIRE DRILL

we had a fire drill
on the 28th of March
in 1960
and it was on Monday
morning

then we had
another fire drill
on the 29th of March
in 1960
but it was on Tuesday
afternoon too

so Mom decided
to Dad
that they take a picture
of Janelle
with a messy face

GRANDPA HAD A TRAILER

Grandpa had a trailer
hitched on his tractor
to give us a ride
on the 7th of August
in 1960

then Aunt Rosella
gave me a drink of water
because I
was so thirsty

then we went off again
but Grandpa held Janelle
when he drove the tractor
on Sunday morning too

but Grandma Lanoue
got the dinner
ready for us then Debbie

made Jim Letourneau laugh
by making
a funny face

MY SILVER CAP

I went to the dentist

on the 2nd of September
in 1960

because I lost
my silver cap

and it was on Friday afternoon
but it was so clear

on that day too

ABOUT INDIANS

we learned about Indians
on the 12th of September
in 1960
and it was on
Monday afternoon
in Mrs. Jepsen's classroom
too

so Mike Dvorak
brought the moccassins
to school
on the 13th of September
in 1960

but it was on Tuesday
morning too

NO TALKING

we had the fire drill
on the 30th of September
in 1960

and it was on
Friday morning

because Mrs. Ryan
told Terry Barker
that there will be

no talking
in the fire drill
too

TERRY BARKER

we had a fire drill
on the 6th of October
in 1960

and it was on Thursday
afternoon

but Terry Barker
hit me

so it was my birthday
then I started crying
on that day

when I came back
to Mrs. Jepsen's classroom
too

FOURTH GRADE READING BOOKS

I went back to school
on the 3rd of November
in 1960

and it was on
Thursday too

but Mrs. Jepsen told me
that they read their story
in fourth grade reading books

except
for me

SUBSTITUTE TEACHER

the substitute teacher
took over
because the real teacher
was not here

on the 21st of November
in 1960

Mom told the substitute teacher
that her mother lives
in Wellington, Kansas

on the 22nd of November
in 1960

when she picked me up
for my speech lessons

THE YEAR of 1961

SPELLING TEST

I didn't go to school
on the 1st of March in 1961
and it was on Wednesday

but I didn't go to school
on the 2nd of March in 1961
because I had a bad cold

then I went back to school
on the 3rd of March in 1961

so everybody got 100
on their spelling test
even me

because I spelled
all the spelling words
right too

MISTAKEN

I was mistaken about
that question

and Mrs. Jepsen asked me
if I read the story

then I said yes
but I should have said
no to her

the first time
on Tuesday morning
in 1961

but it was on the 9th
of May

I think so

THE GREAT BIG MONKEY

we went to the zoo
in Lincoln
to spend Father's Day

on the 18th of June
in 1961
and it was on Sunday

but a great big monkey
spat some water
at Dad

then Kathy Hines
took a picture
of a statue buffalo
on that day

so Janelle
looked at the goats
even Tommy
too

PIONEER VILLAGE

we went
to Pioneer Village
in Minden, Nebraska
with Uncle Andre's
on the 29th of July
in 1961 and it
was on Saturday

then went inside
the building
that has the old stuff
the people used
in those days
of long ago

THE CAR WAS ON FIRE

we went home
on the 13th of August
in 1961

and the car was on fire
when we reached Lincoln

but we went
to the Normans for watermelon

because they invited us over
on that Sunday night

I JUST DON'T UNDERSTAND

I went shopping with Mom
on the 1st of September
in 1961

but she looked
for that song
of "I Just Don't Understand"
on the record
by Ann-Margret
and she couldn't find it

then she asked me
how about that song
of "Does Your Chewing Gum Lose
Its Flavor on the Bed Post Overnight"?

so I told her
no

when I sat in the car
until we got home
too

THERAPY ROOM

I went inside
Mrs. Garnett's therapy room
on the 26th of September
in 1961

and it was on Tuesday
morning too

but Mrs. Brown asked me
what Mom said
about my wet pants
on the same day

at Dr J. P. Lord School

A NAIL

I had a nail
in one of my shoes

on the 27th of September
in 1961

and it was a good thing
that I told my father

on Wednesday morning
but it was David's birthday

too

MOM TOLD ME

Mom told me
that she won't let me
go to school
if I wet me

when I came home
from school
with wet pants

and it was on Tuesday
afternoon

so I typed a letter
to Mrs. Brown

on the 31st of October
in 1961

BAD AS THE KIDS

I really had to go
to the bathroom

and Mrs. Brown told me
that I'm bad as the kids

on the 13th of November
in 1961

at Civic Auditorium
in Dr. J. P. Lord School

so she took me
to the bathroom

but it was on Monday
afternoon

TWO FINGERS

I was in Mrs. Jepsen's
classroom
for fifth grade

and I held up two fingers
that means bathroom

then I asked Debbie
if she wants to play
a game with me

when she came home
from school

on the 28th of November
in 1961

MACARONI & CHEESE

I had macaroni & cheese
at Dr. Lord School

in Civic Auditorium
on the 30th day of November
in 1961

but it was on
Thursday morning

then Steve Sheet
used to know

how to walk

SLOBBY JOES

I had Slobby Joes for lunch
in Civic Auditorium

on the 1st of December
in 1961

and it was on Friday morning
at Dr. Lord School

but it was so cloudy
on that day

then I was in Mrs. Jepsen's
classroom

for fifth grade
too

YOU ARE MY SUNSHINE

Dad sang that song
of "You Are My Sunshine"

like a little girl

on the 4th of December
in 1961

and it was on Monday
morning too

then Grandma Knight
laughed at him

when he got me
in my wheelchair

with braces
on me

THE YEAR of 1962

MY LEFT THUMB NAIL

I pulled
my left thumb nail
on my braces

on the 10th of January
in 1962

and it was on Wednesday
morning too

but it was so clear
on that day

when I was in Mrs. Jepsen's
classroom too

MOM LAUGHED AT ME

Mom laughed at me
on the 29th of January
in 1962

and it was on Monday
morning

because I had
a sad look on my face

then Dad came home
for lunch
on Monday afternoon

so I told him
that I will be good
before supper

BEAUTIFUL MORNING

we sang that song
of "O What a Beautiful Morning"

on the 8th of March
in 1962

and it was on Thursday
afternoon

but it was so cloudy
on that day too

right after
the rest period

MRS. BROWN

Mrs. Brown spanked
Terry Barker
with a ruler
on the 2nd of May
in 1962
and it was on Wednesday
afternoon

so I laughed at that
then she told me
that there is
nothing funny
but she really meant it
too

PEONY PARK

I squirted Dad
with a garden hose
on the 17th of June
in 1962

and it was on Sunday

but it was on Father's Day
then Bill Hines
laughed
even me
in the backyard too

we went to Peony Park
on the 19th of June
in 1962
with the Hines's

and it was on Tuesday
afternoon

then my family went swimming
except for me
even the Hines's

but I watched thm
through the fence
at Peony Park

THE HEN

we rode the 1880 Train
on the 12th of July
in 1962

and it was on Thursday
morning too

but I was on
the end

so we went inside
the building

then the cowboy talked funny
to David

he laughed at the cowboy
because he was funny

we saw the hen
that predicts the weather
like it's gonna be nice

but the hen said yes
by pulling the handle

and the other question
was, is it going to rain?

then the hen said no
so the hen was wrong

because it rained
on that day

DINOSAURS

we got to our tent
even the Hines's
got to their tent

and we just made it
in a nick of time

so we went to a motel
in Cedar Rapids

then we stayed over there
for only two nights

then we went inside
to see dinosaurs

on the 13th of July
in 1962
on Friday morning too

it was so cloudy
on that day

but they are not
real ones

so they took a picture
then
they are so big

RONNIE PUSHED ME

we had a street party
on the 12th of August
in 1962

and it was on Sunday
afternoon

but Vickie had a program
with the kids

like they sang the song
of "The Wells Fargo Wagon"

then Ronnie pushed me
like a hotrod

later on in the night

THE YEAR of 1963

MRS. BREEZKE

Mrs. Breezke asked me
how old I was
and I said 15 years old

on the 25th of January
in 1963

and it was on
Friday morning

but it was so cloudy
on that day too

GRANDMA KNIGHT

we went to see Grandma Knight
in Wellington, Kansas

on the 5th of July
in 1963

and we drove
to Aunt Ida's house
on a farm
in Wellington, Kansas

then she showed
our kids
where the old farm
used to be

except for me
because I
was in the car

JOHN FITZGERALD KENNEDY

John Fitzgerald Kennedy
has been shot
on the 22nd of November
in 1963

and it was on Friday
afternoon

but someone
told Mom
on the telephone

then it was so cloudy
on that day
too

THE YEAR of 1964

NEW YEAR'S RESOLUTIONS

David asked me
what my New Year's resolutions are

and one of my
New Year's resolutions
is to not laugh

then I told Dad
that I will be good
when he gets me up

on the 1st of January
in 1964

and it was on Wednesday
morning too

THE BLACK AND WHITE TELEVISION SET

the black and white television set
came

on the 11th of March
in 1964

but it was on
Wednesday morning

from Magnavox
when I was in this bedroom

doing arithmetic
for school work too

McDONALD'S

we had some hamburgers
at McDonald's

when we drove
to that restaurant

but we ate in the car
on the 30th of May
in 1964

and it was on Saturday
afternoon too

UNCLE WAYNE

we went to Concordia, Kansas
for Carolyn and Adrian's wedding
on the 5th of June in 1964

we stayed at Aunt Rosella's
for two nights

my family went to their wedding
except for me

on the 6th of June in 1964
in Concordia, Kansas

but they got me
right after lunch

there were Evelyn Holinde
with all of her children
except for Kenneth Holinde

and she came out
to say hello to me

Dad went to get some
hamburgers for me

when we went back
to Aunt Rosella's house

and I asked
Uncle Wayne
if he can understand me

then he shook his head
yes

he said that he can
so he
was mistaken

RONNIE

Ronnie put my shoes
on the wrong feet

on the 7th of August
in 1964

and it was on Friday
morning

then they had toast
with milk on it

but on that morning
for breakfast

Ronnie slept with me
on the 8th of August

in 1964
and it was on Saturday
night

but I told him
that I'm so cold

so he turned it off
because I was so cold

on that night

NAME IS JILL

I saw a lady
with real long
straight
hair

name is Jill

on *Loretta Young*
on the 16th of October
in 1964

and it was on Friday
afternoon
at 12:00 pm

WHAT YEAR

Grandpa and Grandma Lanoue
brought Janis over here
on the 18th of October
in 1964

then Grandpa asked me
to see if I know
what year when they moved
in their new house

so I said 1955

while they used to live
on a farm
in Aurora, Kansas

MY NAME IS RICK

Janelle told
that my name is Rick
to Leslie
and it's not Ricky

on the 15th of November
in 1964
and it was on Sunday
afternoon

but it was so cloudy
on that day

then she said Rick
the second time

but she should have said Rick
the first time too

ALL YE FAITHFUL

I asked Mom if she knows
the last verse

to the Christmas song
of "O Come, All Ye Faithful"

on the 4th of December
in 1964

and she said
no to me

but it was on Friday
afternoon too

ANOTHER CHRISTMAS ALBUM

Mom bought another

Christmas album
with Kate Smith

on the 14th of December
in 1964

and it was on Monday
afternoon too

she bought it right after
she pottied me

THE YEAR of 1965

PIRATE SHIP CLUB

David and I
even Janelle
had a pirate ship club

on the 22nd of January
in 1965

but it was so cloudy
on that day

it was on Friday afternoon
when the kids
were home from school

A REAL MEAN LOOK

Janelle gave me
a real mean look

to see if I will get mad
for a test

on the 23rd of February
in 1965

and it was on Wednesday
morning too

JANELLE WAS SEVEN

Janelle was seven years old
on the 7th of November
in 1965

and it was on Sunday

then I gave her
a baton on her birthday
even a Mother Goose album

but she had fried chicken
for her birthday dinner too

so she had a chocolate
birthday cake

with ice cream

I TOLD GRANDMA

I told Grandma Knight
to not put my pajama bottoms
in the drawer

so I can fold them
then put them in

on the 29th of November
in 1965

and it was on Monday
morning too
when we were in the kitchen

if I don't tell her
then she puts it
without being folded

and it's a good thing
that I told her that

BAD THINGS

Mom and Dad took Janelle
to breakfast
on the 4th of December
in 1965

but it was on Saturday
morning

then they bought a Christmas album
with Elvis Presley for me

on the same day
so they left
right after lunch

Janelle wrote bad things
what David said
when they were shopping

so she read the bad things
what David said

to Dad

HAPPY ENDING

I watched the Christmas story
of Rudolf, the Red-Nosed Reindeer
with Burl Ives
telling the story
for the second time

on the 5th of December
in 1965

it was a happy ending
when they took off
on Christmas Eve
and Santa says Merry Christmas

he stopped
for misfit toys

I LAUGHED

I laughed
when I ate my lunch
on that day

but I promised Grandma Knight
that I won't laugh

on the 16th of December
in 1965

and it was on Thursday
afternoon

then I broke my word
to Grandma Knight

I KEEP MY THINGS NEAT

Mom knows
that I keep my things neat

so she told me that
on the 22nd of December
in 1965

and it was on Wednesday
evening
before suppertime
too

SAD

I told David
that I'm sad
on the 23rd of December
in 1965

and it was on
Thursday morning

so I told him
that he don't think
that I keep my things neat

but he knew
that I keep my things neat

when we were in
this bedroom

THE YEAR of 1966

I SAW A GIRL

I saw a girl
with real long
straight
shining
hair

on game number two
name is Arlene

on the program
The Dating Game

on the 19th of April
in 1966

and it was on
Tuesday morning

when it's down

JESUS

I told Jesus
what I will do

on the 20th of May
in 1966

and David smiled at me
on Friday afternoon

but I watched the program
of *Sing Along with Mitch*
that came on television

so we played a game
of dominoes
right after I watched

my favorite
program
too

THE BACK SEAT

we went to Aurora, Kansas
on the 28th of May
in 1966

and it was on Saturday
afternoon

but we stopped
at the restaurant in Fremont

so we stayed for only
two nights

Dad put me in the back seat
of the car
on the 29th of May
in 1966

and it was on
Sunday morning

but I sat in the car
then Gene came to talk to me

so I told Gloria
when her birthday is

she said
right to me

so she told
Aunt Theresa
that I remembered

when her birthday
is

IN OUR BEDS

I told David

that I can't go on a train
without a ticket

and he said
no to me

on the 10th of August
in 1966

but it was on Wednesday
night

when we were in our beds
in this bedroom

SOME TEA

we played dominoes
on the 18th of August
in 1966

and it was on Thursday
night

then Dad wanted Debbie
to make him some tea

so she did
but she was acting up
on that day

he made it himself

so he made me
a glass of ice tea

because he don't like
the way Debbie
was acting

and I don't blame him
for not drinking tea

LONG HAIR OF GIRLS

David and Debbie and Janelle
started school

on the 29th of August
in 1966

but it was on Monday
morning

then Debbie asked me
if I like long hair of girls

so I said yes
to her

REIKO

I saw a lady
whose name is Reiko

and she has real long
straight
shining
hair

but she comes from Japan

then I saw her
on the program

The Merv Griffin Show
at first

since the 8th of November
in 1966

so I came to the den
on Tuesday afternoon

but her hair was down
too

THE TROPHY

David won the trophy
on the 16th of December
in 1966
and it was on Friday
at St. Bernard's School

but he came home
for lunch
then I told him
that I'm sorry

on that morning
so he saw me crying
over a song
of "Don't You Worry If I Can't Sleep"

THE YEAR of 1967

THE NAME OF THE LORD

David and I
were outside
on the 19th of February
in 1967

then we had a family discussion
on Sunday afternoon

but I told Mom
that I don't want David
to take the name of the Lord
in vain

so she agreed with me
on that day too

Mom asked me
if David took the name
of the Lord in vain

on the 26th of February
in 1967

and it was on Sunday
afternoon

but I said no to her
right after lunch

FAMILY MEETING

we had our family meeting
on the 12th of March
in 1967

and it was on Sunday
afternoon

then I discussed
that Janelle borrowed some
of my typing paper

but Mom asked me
if she asked me

so I said no
to her

CREAM CORN

I had cream corn for lunch
on the 31st of March
in 1967

and it was on Monday
afternoon

then I ate
in the diningroom
of the Haven House
on that day

so I sat on the pot
right after lunch

KOOL-AID RABBIT

Ronnie Lickert came over
dressed like a Kool-Aid rabbit

and Marge Lickert
came in the house
on the 18th of May
in 1967

but it was on Thursday
afternoon
right after school

then Janelle didn't do
anything
to make me mad

A SHOW

a neighbor girl
that used to live next door

name is
Dawnie Helm

called me Rick
for the first time
on the 27th of July
in 1967

and it was on Thursday
evening
when she gave a show
for me to watch

in the window

THE BLUE MUSTANG

we got the blue Mustang
on the 8th
of September

in 1967
and it was on Friday
night

so we took a little ride
right after supper
even me too

then we went over
to the Hines's

but we went home
right after
sunset

THE FARM SET

David looked at the farm set
in the catalog
and he asked me
if I want that

but I told him
that I'm too big

then he told me
no I'm not

on the 25th of September
in 1967
so it was on Monday

I told Mom
what David asked me
on the 26th of September
in 1967
and it was on Tuesday

then she agreed with me
by shaking her head
yes on that day

but it was in the morning
when I told her
that I'm too big for that
before lunch

FIRST CHRISTMAS SHOW

I had the first Christmas Show
on Christmas Eve in 1967

and it was on Sunday
afternoon

then I had it
in the afternoon

but the date for that day
was on the 24th of December

so I opened one of my
Christmas presents

so we went to see
the Christmas lights

on Sunday night

THE YEAR of 1968

FLU

Grandma Knight got a letter
from one of her friends

on the 3rd of January
in 1968

the town of Wellington, Kansas
was full of flu
so she told that to David

on the 4th of January
in 1968

then she called Mrs. Hartman
about that
on the telephone

Mom said that word
of flu

on the 15th of January
in 1968

but she shouldn't say that word
because I might get sick

and it was on Monday
night
when we were at the table

in the kitchen too
so we ate our supper

SHE FORGOT

we went over to the Lickerts
to spend a day
at their house

on the 30th of May
in 1968

and it was on Thursday
but is known
as Memorial Day

then we had a picnic
in their backyard

so we showed home movies
in their basement

Marge Lickert asked me
if I want some Kool-Aid
and I said yes to her

then she forgot
to give me some Kool-Aid

on that day
too

BIRTHDAY CARD

I got another birthday card
from Rita Wolf

on the 9th of October
in 1968

and it was on Tuesday
afternoon

so Debbie played a game
of Scribbage with me
right after school

even Janelle played a game
of Po-Ke-No with me too

I typed another thank you letter
to Grandpa Lanoue

to tell him thank you
for the birthday card

and I wanted him
to tell Grandma thank you
for the birthday card

because it saves me
a lot of time
too

SO BLUE

Dad went to the store
to get some ice cream

on the 20th of October
in 1968

and I was so blue
on that night

but it was on Sunday
then they watched the Olympics

on TV

DEBBIE TOLD ME TO RELAX

Mom and Dad
went to a Halloween party

on the 26th of October
in 1968

but I had to dirty
on that night

so Debbie told me
to relax

then I shouldn't eat
four hamburgers

too

A PICTURE OF A TREE

I colored a picture
of a tree
on a piece of paper

on the 13th of December
in 1968

to give it to Mom
for Christmas

then I told her
that Christmas will be
on Friday in 1970

and it was
but I was right

before supper
too

PLAY ALONG

Janelle told Mom
that some of the girls
think that Christmas
really means Santa Claus
to them

on the 19th of December
in 1968
when we ate our lunch

and Mom told her
to play along with them
on Thursday afternoon
too

I told Dad
what Janelle told Mom
on the 21st of December
in 1968
when we decorated
the Christmas tree

and it was on Saturday
in the livingroom
too

THE YEAR of 1969

BLUE LITTLE PIANO

Grandma taught me how to play
that Christmas song
of "Joy to the World"
on the 12th of January
in 1969

and it was on Sunday
morning
in the kitchen

she also taught me how to play
that song
of "Jesus Loves Me"
on the 13th of January
in 1969

and it was on Monday
morning
on the blue little piano
too

WOE IS ME

Janelle didn't want me
to say

woe is me

on the 24th of January
in 1969

and it was on
Friday morning

too

DAD TOOK THE RECORD PLAYER

Dad took the record player
to get fixed

on the 25th of January
in 1969

and it was on Saturday
afternoon

but my family
went to confession

except me
on the same day

so Janelle asked me
what is the zip code number
for Wellington, Kansas?

then I typed nice things
about Janelle

on a piece of typewriter paper
on Saturday night

HAPPY

I told Janelle
that I'm happy

and she
asked me why

on the 14th of June
in 1969

HALF OF MY BED

I told Mom
that I made
the half of my bed

and she said
good for you
to me

then she asked me
if David made
his own bed

and I said no

on the 4th of July
in 1969
but it was on
Friday afternoon

so we went to the drive-in
to watch a movie
right after supper
too

DAVID'S RECORDS

Debbie wanted me
to play David's records
without his permission

so David got home
then he was so mad at me

on the 1st of September
in 1969

and it was on Monday
morning
before lunchtime

but I went outside
on the same day
right after lunch too

ACNE

Debbie told me
that grass makes the acne
go away

on the 7th of September
in 1969

and I laughed at that one
too because
I was outside then Mom
was outside with me

in the front yard
so I asked God

where David was
on the same day

THE AIR CONDITIONER

Mom asked me

what year when we got
the air conditioner

so I said 1963
then she checked it up
to see if I'm right

and sure enough
I'm right

on the 14th of September
in 1969

but it was on Sunday
evening too

A CHRISTMAS SHOW

I had a Christmas show
on the 21st of December
in 1969

then David was
Baby Jesus
by wearing diapers

on the same day
that made Grandma Knight
laugh so hard

then Debbie was Mary
or Janelle was an angel
in that Christmas play

on Sunday afternoon
in the new part
of downstairs

THE YEAR of 1970

GARY SADIL

I met Gary Sadil
on the 16th of January
in 1970

for the first time
and it was on Friday night

when he got some runzas
with David

but he came by
for the first time

KIM RAUHUT

I met Kim Rauhut
on the 7th of March
in 1970

and it was on Saturday
night when David
had a party

David invited all
of his friends
over for a party
on the same night

and he borrowed
the old record player
for his party

he returned it
on the 8th of March
in 1970

and it was on
Sunday night

so he told me
thank you too

THE NAUGHTY WORD

Debbie wanted me to say
the naughty word

by giving us a clue
on the 2nd of May
in 1970

and it was on Saturday
morning

then Janelle won
because she
said the naughty word

that rhymes with cart
but it starts
with the letter F

I lost because I didn't say
the naughty word

then Mom was so proud of me
that morning

CHRIS BLAKE

Chris Blake locked the kids
in the bathroom

so I tried to rescue
the kids

then Pat Hines
came in

on the 7th of May
in 1970

and it was on Thursday
night too

JANIS CAME

Janis came here
with her roommate

name is
Sue Newton

on the 20th of June
in 1970

and it was on Saturday

then Sue asked me
to see if I know
when her birthday is

so I said
the 30th of May

but she said
right to me

before they went
to the races

DAVID'S BED

I made the half
of David's bed
but he messed it
all up

so I told Mom
what David did

on the 25th of June
in 1970

and it was on
Thursday morning
too

TWO RIVERS

we all went
to the Two Rivers
on the 28th of June
in 1970

and it was so clear
on that day
but it was so hot
on that day

then I saw a lady
with real
long
hair
which it was down
on that day

when she was walking
along the beach

DISC JOCKEY

I corrected the disc jockey
on KOIL radio

about what year for the
song of "Cherish"

on the 28th of July
in 1970

and it was on Tuesday
afternoon
before lunch

so I told David
about that

then he
told Mom too

PANCAKES

I had some pancakes
for lunch

so Gary Sadil
gave some pancakes
to Skippy

on the 11th of August
in 1970

so I told Mom
when she came home

and it was on Tuesday
afternoon too

LIKE THE BEATLES

I told Mom
that I don't want to look
awful like the Beatles

on the 19th of September
in 1970

so Mom agreed with me
and it was on Saturday
evening

then Dad
gave me a haircut

even a bath
too

AUNT ROSELLA

Aunt Theresa came
to Aurora, Kansas
on the 29th of November
in 1970

and it was on Sunday
morning

which Uncle Leo played a game
of dominoes with me

then he asked me
how many dominoes
do we draw

so I said seven
but he repeated to make sure
if I said seven

I was so honest with him
by saying yes
on that day

and it was so clear
on that day
at Grandpa's house

then we stopped
at Aunt Theresa's house

then I asked Aunt Rosella

if she will find me
a girl with real long
straight
shining
hair

but I was silly
on that day

THE YEAR of 1971

SO AFRAID

Mom took me
to the bathroom

on the 8th of March
in 1971

and it was on Monday
morning

then I started to cry
because I am so afraid

that Mom would be
so mad at me

so she asked me
real nice
to make the half
of both beds

which I probably did

WITH A SMILE

Janelle fixed me
some pancakes

on the 22nd of May
in 1971

so I told her
serve with a smile

then she repeated it
to make sure if I said that

which I did

AGGRAVATION

Debbie told me to type it
on a piece of white
typewriter paper

if I beat her in a game
of Aggravation
then she will bite my finger

then it was stupid for me
to type that
so I threw it away

on the 29th of June
in 1971

and it was on Tuesday
morning too

A PICNIC

I went on a picnic
on the 8th of July

in 1971
with Kim and David

then Saucy licked my hand
so it made me laugh
real hard
all the time

except for eating
our lunch

then we took a walk
right after lunch
too

TONY LETOURNEAU

Tony Letourneau
got killed

on the 20th of July
in 1971

and it was on Tuesday

but Kim Rauhut came
then she gave David

a Beatles album
to play it
on the same day

ROCK CONCERT

we went to the rock concert
on the 1st of August
in 1971

but Dad told me
that they throw some rocks

then it made us laugh
on that night

and it was on Sunday
right after supper

so we went to Kim's house
on that Sunday night

but we got home
late because
it was so late

too

KIM CAME OVER

Kim came over
on the 21st of August
in 1971

and it was on Saturday
night

then I asked Jesus
to make Saucy better

so she told me
thank you too

Kim Rauhut gave me
a drink of ice water

at Donna Philip's house
then she made me choke

but she told me
that she's sorry

so I told her
that I forgive her

which she told me
thank you

to me

MR. RAUHUT

David and I went
to Kim Rauhut's house

but Mr. Rauhut played
the songs of Christmas
on the organ

on the 22nd of August
in 1971

then Kim told me
that I made her happy
by being her friend

with a nice smile
on her face

so it was a clear day
too

DAVID GOT HURT

David got hurt
at the gymnastic tryouts

on the 28th of August
in 1971

and it was on Saturday
night

but Kim told him
to be careful

so I told her
that she has nice smiles
on the telephone

then she thought
that I'm just kidding

but I really mean
what I told her

HAIRCUT

Kim Rauhut thought
that I would be mad at her

and I said no to her
on the telephone

on the 1st of October
in 1971

and it was on Friday
evening

then she told me
to grow my hair long

so I can't make
that promise

Dad gave me a haircut

on the 2nd of October
in 1971

SILLY

Janelle told me
that I should type her
a thank you letter

to tell her thank you
for the birthday card
that she gave me

on the 7th of October
in 1971

but it was on
Thursday morning

then Mom knew
that it was silly

A REAL NICE YOUNG LADY

I talked to Kim Rauhut
on the telephone

on the 20th of October
in 1971

and it was on Wednesday
night too

but I like her
very much

but I always will
like her

because she is a real
nice young lady

for a real long time

SO ICKY

I talked to Kim Rauhut
on the telephone
in the girls' bedroom

on the 16th of November
in 1971

and she told me
that she can't stand David
because he's so icky

but it was on Tuesday
afternoon

AS THE WORLD TURNS

I started to cry

when I heard the opening
theme song
of *As the World Turns*

on the 1st of December
in 1971

and it was on Wednesday
afternoon too

A LETTER TO SANTA CLAUS

I typed a letter to Santa Claus
on the 14th of December
in 1971

because Debbie wanted me
to do that

but Mom and Grandma
laughed real hard
on Tuesday morning

then it was on
a cloudy day

so I typed a letter
to Santa Claus
to ask him for

a green booger picker

MRS. RAUHUT

Kim Rauhut was here
and she ate supper with us

so we went out
for a ride
on the 23rd of December
in 1971

then Grandma went
with us

to Kim Rauhut's house
even me too

Mrs. Rauhut said merry Christmas
to me in Spanish
on Thursday night

but she came downstairs
to see me

then I taught her how to play
that Christmas song
of "Joy to the World"
on the organ

Dad gave me a bath
on the same night

THE YEAR of 1972

FUNNY THINGS

David said
the funny things
when he took me
to the bathroom

and it made
Grandma Knight
laugh

on the 25th
of January
in 1972

but it was on
Tuesday afternoon
too

THE AIRPLANES

David gave himself a haircut
and a shave too
on the 4th of February
in 1972

but it was on Friday
afternoon

so I asked if he
do me a favor

then I named a favor
that I want him to do
for me
on Friday night too

I want him to give me
a ride was the favor
of the 5th of February
in 1972

so he gave me a ride
and it was on Saturday
afternoon

then we drove to the airport
to watch
the airplanes

WILL ROGERS

I watched the show
of Will Rogers
on the TV

on the 24th of February
in 1972
and it was on Thursday
night

but he is a funny man

so David told me
that I never know

if the people are kidding
or serious

I CONFESSED

David pushed me
up Manderson Street

on the 5th of March
in 1972

and it was on Sunday
afternoon

so I went to church
on that day

I confessed my sins
inside Saint Bernard's church

so I went to communion
on the same day

LOTTA PHATT

I stayed home
all day long
on the 8th of April
in 1972

and it was on Saturday
too

but I got a letter
from Lotta Phatt
on the same day
in the mail

Lotta Phatt called me up
on the telephone
on the 9th of April
in 1972

and it was on Sunday
evening

I stayed home
on the 10th of April
in 1972

and it was on Monday
too

MOO AND RICOCHET

Kim's name was Moo
but my name was Ricochet

for cowboys' first names
while we were riding along
in the car

but David asked Kim
what name that she wants to have

then she said Moo

so he asked me
what name that I want to have

which I said Ricochet

on the 15th of April
in 1972

it was on Saturday
too

WHEN HER LIPS ARE CLOSE

David and I took a ride

on the 15th of April
in 1972

but it was on Saturday
afternoon

then Kim was in the middle
of the front seat

so I told Kim
no matter if she is ugly
or not

which I like her
with whole bunches

because she is a nice
young lady

she smiled when her lips
are close

too

POKER PARTY

Dad went
to the poker party

on the 5th of May
in 1972

but Dad put me to bed
early on Friday night too

then David said
that he will find a girl

with real long
straight
shining
hair

for me

UNFAIR PARENTS

I told Mom and Dad
that they are unfair with me
about not letting me
call Kim Rauhut

on the 22nd of May
in 1972

then they won't
listen to me

so David agreed
with me

I put Unfair Parents
on a piece of white
typewriter paper

so David hung it up
with scotch tape
on their bedroom door

TALKING LIKE AN OLD LADY

David was talking
like an old lady

on the 23rd of May
in 1972

and it was on Tuesday
morning

but he was talking
like Joe Slick too

Kim knows
that Mom and Dad
are unfair

I told David
that I will let my son
to call Kim Rauhut

but he tapped me
on my shoulder

on that Tuesday
afternoon

YELLING

I typed Mom a note
because she has been gone

on the 29th of June
in 1972
and it was on Thursday

but Kim was sad
when she came in the car

because David
was yelling at Kim

then we went
to some kind of park

on Thursday evening
too

IF I WERE KIM

I told Mom
that you know about Kim

but she didn't tell David
to get a haircut

and she should tell him
to get a haircut

on the 6th of July
in 1972

if I were Kim
then I will find myself

a boyfriend
with short hair

and if I were Kim
then I will tell him to go

to the barber shop

KIM CAME OVER

Kim came over to see
the gerbils

on the 13th of July
in 1972

and it was on Thursday
afternoon

but Kim got a letter
from David

so she called Mom
that David hitchhiked

to Wellington, Kansas
on the telephone

but she was darn mad
at him for that too

David came back here
on the 14th of July

and it was on Friday
morning

when I was in bed

CROSSROADS

I went for a ride
on the 29th of July
in 1972

and I saw a girl
with real long
straight
shining
hair

when she walked
the front side
of the Crossroads

but we waited for Debbie
to come out

then it was on Saturday
night too

BRAINWASHED

Janelle told Mom
that she
had brainwashed me

on the 31st of August
in 1972

and it was on Thursday
before supper
too

THOSE WERE THE DAYS

I started school
on the 2nd of October
in 1972

and it was on Monday
morning too

but Joe Mason
came here to get me

because I was the first one
to pick up too

~~Mary Beth Mowry~~ the name
that Mom don't
want me to mention

was in charge of the art
and of the exercise activities
in those days

then she used to remember
my name

but those were the days

OUIJA BOARD

a crippled young boy
that can't talk

and he can use
a Ouija board

name is
Patrick

but he asked me
if my name is Bill

so I point to that word
of no
because that is the truth

on the 11th of October
in 1972

but it was on Wednesday
morning too

I HELPED

I helped the same lady out
that Mom don't
want me to mention

on the 16th of October
in 1972

and Steve Sheet
came to school
for the first time

then I typed nice things
about Mrs. Garnett
so she read it

which made her
so happy too

MOM WAS SO PROUD

I wanted Janelle
to tell me thank you
to me

in a nice tone
of her voice

on the 28th of October
in 1972

and it was on Saturday
afternoon

but I controlled
my temper

then Mom was
so proud of me

MY LEFT HAND

we had art

on the 7th of November
in 1972

and it was on Tuesday
morning

then Judy told me
to use my left hand

but the other lady
told her

that I can't use
my left hand

so she forgot

THERAPY

I was in the teacher's office
and she told me
let me shut the door

because there was
a lot of noise

so she closed the door
on the 29th of November
in 1972

but it was on Wednesday
morning too

Gary Golberg sang
"We Wish You a Donald Olson"

and "O Come, All Ye
Lori Lancasters"

on the 30th of November
in 1972

but it was on Thursday
afternoon

then Doug asked me
if I took some therapy

so I said yes
to him

which he asked me
what I will do

I said walking

so he repeated to make sure
if I said that

and I said yes
to him

JANELLE WAS HELPING

Janelle was helping me
wrapping
the Christmas presents

on the 24th of December
in 1972

but she asked me
where is her Christmas present

so I said shhhh
to her
because I really want
it to be a surprise

then I told Dad
what Janelle asked me

I told the truly meaning
of Christmas
on the same day

but it was in the night time
so Loretta was here
on Christmas Eve

even Pat and big Bill
with all of their children

THE YEAR of 1973

A JOB

I told David
that I want a job

on the 2nd of January
in 1973

and it was on Wednesday
morning

but my sisters told me
that some lady

was at the front door
on the same day

so I know it was in
the afternoon

BAD THINGS

Gary Goldberg told Larry
to watch his language

and he said God damn
to him

on the 19th of January
in 1973

and it was on Friday
afternoon

I have been
so good here

about not bringing up
bad things

so I won't type about that
on a piece
of typewriter paper

MOVEMENT ACTIVITIES

I put my hand
on Steve Sheet's face
to see if he likes it

on the 6th of February
in 1973

and it was on Tuesday
afternoon

but it was so clear
on that day too

during the movement
activities

BEATRICE

I went to school
on the 1st of March
in 1973

and it was on Thursday
but it was so cloudy
on that day too

I also went to school
on the 2nd of March
in 1973

and it was on Friday
but it was so cloudy
on that day

then the lady
that Mom don't want me
to mention
went to Beatrice, Nebraska

I stayed home
on the 3rd of March
in 1973
and it was on Saturday

but Mom fixed me
some lunch on that day

then she stayed
in Beatrice all day too

she came back to Omaha
on the 4th of March
in 1973

and it was on Sunday

THE ELECTRICITY

the electricity went off
on the 8th of March
in 1973

and it was on Thursday
morning about ten

then Gary Goldberg
was gone that day

so we went home
on the same day too

but Mom lit a match
on that afternoon

to see where the urinal was
before lunchtime

A LESSON

I asked the lady
which one does she
like the best
and she said me

on the 14th of March
in 1973

and it was on Wednesday
morning too
before lunchtime

Steve Sheet put his finger
in my mouth
on the same day

so I bit his finger
to teach him a lesson too

right after lunch
then the lady can't blame me
for biting his finger

A HOSE AND A FUNNEL

Mom had
a hose and a funnel
for me

with a bottle
to pee in it

then she put it
in the closet of mine

on the 16th of March
in 1973

but it was on
Friday morning

SILENT

Debbie brushed my hair
on the 24th of April
in 1973

and it was on Tuesday
morning too

then Dad came home
for lunch
on the same day

Debbie sang
that Christmas song
of "Silent Night"

with saying
the naughty word

BAD HEADACHE

Mom had a bad headache

on the 12th of May
in 1973

and it was on Saturday
evening

so I rubbed her head
on the same day

on the back porch

THAT LADY

I typed a letter
to that lady

that Mom don't want me
to mention her name

on the 16th of May
in 1973

and it was on Wednesday
night

I was so happy to see
the lady

that Mom don't want me
to mention her name

on the 25th of May
in 1973

and it was on Friday
but it was so clear

on that day
too

I BELIEVE GARY

I told David
that I believe Gary

when he told me
that the lady will come

that Mom don't want me
to mention her name

so he tapped me
on my shoulder

on the 14th of June
in 1973

and it was on
Thursday too

THOSE WERE THE DAYS

Debbie bought me a record
called "Those Were the Days"

on the 22nd of June
in 1973
and it was on Friday
night

but it is a 45 rpm record

I like the record
that Debbie bought me

so I played it
on the 23rd of June
in 1973

and it was on Saturday
too

THE MATCH GAME

I let Mom help me
play solitaire

on the 14th of August
in 1973

and it was on Tuesday
morning too

then I watched
a TV game show
with Gene Rayburn

so there was a lady
that has real long
straight
shining
hair

on *The Match Game*

MOM TOLD GARY SADIL

Dad got me up
on the 2nd of September
in 1973

and it was on Sunday
morning too

then Mom told Gary Sadil
that I want a girl

with real long
straight
shining
hair

on Sunday night

DRILL TEAM PRACTICE

David and I had a picnic
in our backyard
with Kim Rauhut

on the 3rd of September
in 1973

but it was on Monday
afternoon too

then I told Janelle
that I love her

so we went to Janelle's
drill team practice
on Monday night

which I sat in the car

HOW CAN I TELL HIM?

I asked Mom
how can I tell him
without hurting his feelings

that his hair
looks awful

on the 3rd of October
in 1973

and it was on Wednesday
morning

MOM'S PURSE

Dad was looking
in Mom's purse

on the 8th of November
in 1973

and it was on Thursday
morning too

but I said
none of your business
to Dad

so I asked Mom
right?

which she said
right
to me

PROMISE

Dad wanted me
to promise him

to not wet my pants

on the 10th of November
in 1973

and it was on Saturday
night too

GRANNY SLICK

David was talking
like Granny Slick

when he took me
to the bathroom

on the 13th of November
in 1973

and it was on Tuesday
afternoon

LAUGHING

Dad and I were laughing
when Mom

took the parts of the stove
to the bathtub

on the 27th of November
in 1973

but it was on Tuesday
morning too

then Mom started laughing
at that one too

so Grandma asked Mom
what is funny

THE YEAR of 1974

DAVID TOLD THEM

Mom and Dad
came back from the trip
to California

on the 11th of January
in 1974

but it was on Friday
night

then David told them
that I was terrible

in the mornings
too

OVER THE RAINBOW

The Wizard of Oz
came on

the 17th of February
in 1974

and it was on Sunday
night

but it was in color
when Dorothy

went over the rainbow
too

APRIL FOOL

I told Mom
that I got a letter
from that lady

that Mom don't want me
to mention

on the 1st of April
in 1974

and it was on Monday
morning

but she said
April fool
to me

THE PETERSONS' BACKYARD

Dad didn't go to work
on the 23rd of April
in 1974

and it was on Tuesday

so Mom looked out
the kitchen window
but she saw

the Petersons' backyard

then they don't care
what their backyard
looks like

PERMANENT

I told Dad
that I'm so blue
on the 25th of April
in 1974

and it was on Thursday
night
when he put me
to bed

so he asked me
why
on the same night
too

Loretta came over
on the 26th of April
in 1974

and it was on Friday
afternoon
for a permanent

so I told her
that I was so blue
on that same day
too

A CAR FULL OF PEOPLE

David and I
had a car full of people
on the 23rd of May
in 1974

but it was on Thursday
evening

then we ate our supper
before we went
to see a movie too
on that night

we saw
Butch Cassidy and the Sundance Kid
at a drive-in theater

David thinks
that the program
of *The Brady Bunch*
is Sicko Bunch

on the 24th of May
in 1974

and it was on Friday
morning too

WESTROADS

David and I
went to get Kim

on the 20th of June
in 1974
but it was on Thursday

so we went to Westroads
to get Mom's birthday present

then we ate
at the Westroads
on that day

which I saw a girl
with real long
straight
shining
hair

ELMWOOD PARK

I went to a rock concert
on the 23rd of June
in 1974
with Kim and David

but it was on Sunday night
at Elmwood Park

so I saw a young lady
with real long
straight
shining
hair

when it's down

then I pushed myself
across the grass

THAT'LL BE THE DAY

Janelle said
that she will hire me
to clean up her house

and I said
that'll be the day

on the 18th of October
in 1974

but it was on Friday
night too

THE YEAR of 1975

LOST IN THE SNOW

we had a big blizzard
on the 10th of January
in 1975

and it was on Friday
too

then Dad's car was lost
in the blizzard too

so Dad was lost
in the snow

on that day

RESOLUTIONS FOR JANELLE

I typed the New Year's resolutions
for Janelle

on the 11th of January
in 1975

and it was on Saturday
afternoon

so Dad put it
in her bedroom too

Janelle tore up
the piece of typewriter paper

on the 12th of January
in 1975

and it was on Sunday
too

BENSON WOMEN'S REPUBLICAN CLUB

I typed the roster
for Benson Women's Republican Club

on the 8th of March
in 1975
and it was on Tuesday

but it was so cloudy
on that day

then I met a nice man
from Dr J. P. Lord School

on Tuesday morning
too

UNDER MY ARMS

I typed a letter to Grandma
on the 22nd of May
in 1975

and it was on Thursday
morning too

so Dad washed
under my arms
on that night too

LITTLE KIDS

David and Janelle took me
to Creighton
for a concert

on the 3rd of August
in 1975

but it was on Sunday
evening

then we stopped
at Dairy Queen
to get some ice cream

so the little kids
laughed at me

when David
was feeding me

RICK'S VAN

Mom decorated the van
and she put
Rick's Van

on the 5th of August
in 1975

but it was on Tuesday
morning

so Dad gave me a bath
on the same night
too

LIZ LEFTWICH

Liz Leftwich brushed
her long hair
for me to see

on the 12th of August
in 1975

and it was on Tuesday
morning

then we went fishing
on the same day

so Dick threw a wet balloon
at Liz Leftwich

on Tuesday night
at the camp too

SHAME ON ME

I gave Debbie a T-shirt
that has
Shame on Me

on the 30th of October
in 1975

and it was on Thursday
night

right after supper
too

THE HOSPITAL IN WELLINGTON

we went to see
Grandma Knight

on the 26th of November
in 1975

and it was so late
when we got to
Wellington, Kansas

then Tim drove
some of the way
on Wednesday night

but Dad carried me
inside her house
all by himself too

he spent all day
on Thanksgiving Day
in the hospital
in Wellington, Kansas

on the 27th of November
in 1975

then Mom was feeding me
some pumpkin pie too

but Janelle
took a picture of me

on Thursday afternoon
too

HALF OF HER SANDWICH

Fran Boyce gave me
the half of her sandwich

on the 11th of December
in 1975

and it was on Thursday
afternoon

but it was so cloudy
on that day too

THE YEAR of 1976

I ASKED GOD

Adrian gave me
a *Grease* record

on the 1st of March
in 1976

and it was on Monday
morning too

but it was so cloudy
on that day

then I asked God
if I will get a letter
from the lady

which I told Debbie
what God told me

on Monday night

I WAS CRYING

I was crying

on the 20th of June
in 1976

and it was on Sunday
morning

but it was so clear
on that day

too

TALENT SHOW

we had a talent show
on the 21st of July
in 1976

and it was on Wednesday
night

but I sang
"Those Were ther Days"
for my number

too

LETTERS

I typed another letter
to David and Elly
on the 26th of July
in 1976

but it was on Monday
night too

I typed a letter
to Cheryl Ann Hebert
on the 27th of July
in 1976

and it was on Tuesday
too

I retyped a letter
to Cheryl
on the 28th of July
in 1976

and it was on Wednesday
too

so Dad was working late
on that night

so I took myself
to the bathroom

THE FLY

Janelle told the fly
to leave her alone

on ther 2nd of August
in 1976

and it was on Monday
morning too

so she swatted
the fly

on the same morning

IN THE CAR

my family went to church

on the 8th of August
in 1976

and it was on Sunday
morning

so I sat in the car
on the same morning

too

PAGE NUMBER ONE

I typed page number one

on the 30th of August
in 1976

and it was on Monday
night

but it was so starry
on that night

too

MY RIGHT ARM

I told my right arm
to stay down

on the 24th of September
in 1976

and it was on Friday
afternoon too

WHAT HAPPENED

I wast typing
what happened
in 1959

in the middle of the month
of October
in 1976

and it was on Monday
too

EPSOM SALT

I told Mom
that one of the counselors

brushed my teeth
with Epsom salt

on the 3rd of November
in 1976

and it was on Wednesday
afternoon too

LIKE A MAN

Tim told me
to act like a man

on the 20th of November
in 1976

and it was on Saturday
morning too

ALBERTY

Grandpa called me Ricky
so I called him Alberty

to get even with him

on the 28th of November
in 1976

but it was on Sunday
morning too

REPEAT

Mom don't want me
to repeat things

on the 30th of December
in 1976

and it was on Thursday
evening too

THE YEAR of 1977

NO LUNCH

Grandma knows
that I have to eat

and she didn't fix me
no lunch

on the 14th of January
in 1977

but it was on Friday
afternoon too

FREIGHT TRAIN

I typed all the words
to the song

of "Frieght Train"
for Kim
so she can sing that song

on the 26th of March
in 1977
and it was on Sunday

too

SHRINE CIRCUS

I didn't go
to the Shrine Circus

on the 20th of April
in 1977

and it was on Wednesday
afternoon too

THE BONNET

Bob Campbell

put the bonnet
on my head

so Marge laughed
at what Bob did

on the 5th of May
in 1977

and it was on Thursday
morning too

at Echo School

ROOM NUMBER FIVE

we went to Wayne, Nebraska

on the 28th of May
in 1977 except for Janelle

so I saw my nephew
name is Jeff

on Saturday night too
I went to the hospital again

on the 29th of May
in 1977

and it was on Sunday
afternoon too

so I went to the nursing home
for the second time

then Tim put me
in room number five

ROOM NUMBER 32

my parents took me to Wayne

on the 5th of August
in 1977

so they took me
to Tim's nursing home
on Friday night

then he put me
in the room number 32
for the third time

I met a girl
name is Kathy

on the 6th of August
in 1977

and it was on Saturday
morning

but it was so cloudy
on that morning

then a nurse forgot
to give me my pill

AH COO-COO

I said ah coo-coo
to Jeff

to make him smile
at me

on the 26th of September
in 1977

and it was on Monday
evening too

Jeff said
O
to me

on the 27th of September
in 1977

and it was on Tuesday
evening

OTHER PEOPLE'S ROOMS

I told Tim that I can't go
in other people's rooms

on the 16th of November
in 1977

and it was on Wednesday
afternoon too

THE YEAR of 1978

KINGS AROUND THE CORNER

Grandma played
kings around the corner
with us

on the 12th of January
in 1978

and it was on Thursday
afternoon too

but Debbie told me
that she loves me

on the same night

POOR PEOPLE

I watched the TV program
where there were poor people

all around the world

on the 18th of March
in 1978

and it was on Saturday
night too

JEFF WAS A MONKEY

Jeff was a monkey
on the 28th of June

in 1978
and it was on Wednesday
morning

too

SO FUNNY

Tim was so funny
on the 18th of November
in 1978

and it was on Saturday
but he thought
that I'm his mother-in-law

when he answered
the telephone

then I told him
who I am
on the same day too

THE YEAR of 1979

STROLLING

I listened to my favorite song
of "Strolling through the Park"

on the 9th of January
in 1979

and it was on Tuesday
morning too

I GOT EVEN WITH DAVID

I got even with David
on the 26th of January
in 1979

and it was on Friday
morning too

I told Elly
that I will talk
like Granny Clampett

on the 4th of February
in 1979

and it was on Sunday
afternoon too

MY WISH

my wish came true

on the 6th of March
in 1979

and it was on
Tuesday morning

too

MY WHISKERS

David told Bryan
that my whiskers are thorns

on the 7th of April
in 1979

and it was on Saturday
morning too

when we went to Wayne,
Nebraska

to have our pictures
taken

so we went
to the studio
on the same day

then we were tired
on Saturday night

LIKE JESUS

David made me laugh
by talking like Jesus

on the 22nd of April
in 1979

and it was on Sunday
morning too

then David gave me a walk
on the same day

so it was in
the afternoon
too

A DOLLAR BILL

Grandma Lanoue
came in my bedroom

and she gave me
a dollar bill

on the 1st of May
in 1979

but it was on Tuesday
morning too

then Mom took Grandma Lanoue
to the bus depot

on the same day

COLLEEN'S BAPTISM

we went to Wayne, Nebraska
on the 6th of May

in 1979
for Colleen's baptism

and it was on Sunday
morning

so we got up real early
on that morning too

JEFF PRETENDED

Jeff pretended
that he shot me

on the 26th of May
in 1979

and it was on Saturday
afternoon too

ALICE WARREN

Alice Warren asked me
what kind of pop
do I want

so I said root beer
to her

on the 5th of October
in 1979

and it was on Friday
morning too

Alice thought
that we are getting
married

on the 6th of October
in 1979

and it was on
Saturday afternoon

too

NOTHING

I didn't do nothing

on the 30th of October
in 1979

and it was on Tuesday
but it was so cloudy

on that day too

TOO FULL

I was too full

on the 22nd of November
in 1979

and it was on Thursday
known as

Thanksgiving Day too

THE YEAR of 1980

JANELLE

Janelle told me
good morning

on the 8th of January
in 1980

and it was on Tuesday
morning too

I told Janelle
that she is a pretty
good sister

on the 9th of January
in 1980
and it was Wednesday

night too

1ST OF APRIL

I told Grandma
that I was Aunt Ida

on the 1st of April
in 1980

and it was on Tuesday
morning too

but it was so cloudy
on that day too

DICK AND I

Dick and I don't mind

if we didn't go
to the Shrine Circus

on the 15th of April
in 1980

but it was on Tuesday
afternoon too

LIVER SAUSAGE

Mom told Janelle

to fix me two
liver sausage sandwiches

on the 23rd of April
in 1980

and it was on Wednesday
afternoon too

COLLEEN STANDS

Colleen stands
and she walks alone

on the 15th of July
in 1980

and it was on Tuesday
night too

BUTTERBALL

Janelle brought home
a butterball turkey

on the 28th of August
in 1980

and it was on Thursday
evening too

then Loretta came over
on the same night

BAD NEWS

Dad gave me a bath
on the 8th of September
in 1980

and it was on Monday
night

then Aunt Angeline
called Mom
on that night too

so she told her
the bad news

we went to Concordia,
Kansas
on the 10th of September

in 1980
and it was on Wednesday
afternoon too

then I went inside
Aunt Theresa's house
on that night too

I went to the funeral
on the 11th of September
in 1980

and it was on Thursday
morning too

THE YEAR of 1981

CRYSTAL GAYLE

I watched the lady
that has real long
straight
shining
hair

and her name
is Crystal Gayle

on the 30th of January
in 1981

but it was on Friday
night too

BRYAN WAS SINGING

Bryan was singing
underneath my bed

on the 14th of February
in 1981

but it was on Saturday
evening too

GETTING ALONG WITH JANELLE

Mom told me

that I was getting along
with Janelle

on the 4th of March
in 1981

and it was on
Wednesday too

JANELLE MOVED OUT

Janelle moved out
of this house

on the 1st of August
in 1981

but it was on Saturday
too

Janelle came over here
for supper

on the 5th of August
in 1981

and it was on Wednesday
night too

GARY SADIL'S WEDDING

David came up here
for Gary Sadil's wedding

on the 13th of November
in 1981

and it was on Friday
night

but he drove to Lincoln
too

THE YEAR of 1982

DEBBIE'S KIDS

Debbie's kids helped Mom
to make
chocolate chip cookies

on the 29th of January
in 1982

and it was on Friday
morning too

A PIECE OF CANDY

Janelle came in
my bedroom

on the 15th of February
in 1982

and it was on Monday
night

to give me
a piece of candy

too

DAN JOSEPH REEDER

I met Dan Joseph Reeder
on the 13th of March
in 1982

and it was on Saturday
afternoon

but it was so clear
on that day

then Mom went to play
bridge with Dad
on the same night

Janelle took Dan
to the airport
on the 14th of March

in 1982
and it was on Sunday
too

COCK-A-DOODLE-DOO

I said
cock-a-doodle-doo

on the 20th of March
in 1982

and it was on
Saturday

then I went for a ride
even Grandma

right after lunch
too

MOM ASKED

Mom asked me
what year
Grandpa Lanoue died

on the 26th of May
in 1982

and it was on Wednesday
afternoon too

then I said 1978
to her

A REAL GOOD IDEA

Mom had
a real good idea

for me to quit typing
the history

when I reach the month
of December in 1981

on the 2nd of April
in 1982

and it was on Friday
afternoon

A PROGRAM ABOUT A LITTLE GIRL

I saw a program
about a little girl

with real long
straight
shining
hair

but it
was in braids

on the 30th of December
in 1982

and it was Thursday night
too

www.ingramcontent.com/pod-product-compliance
Lightning Source LLC
LaVergne TN
LVHW051515070426
835507LV00023B/3130